# LIVE IT:
# FAIRNESS

## NATALIE HYDE

# Crabtree Publishing Company
www.crabtreebooks.com

**Author**: Natalie Hyde
**Coordinating editor**: Bonnie Dobkin
**Publishing plan research and development**:
   Sean Charlebois, Reagan Miller
   Crabtree Publishing Company
**Editor**: Reagan Miller
**Proofreader**: Crystal Sikkens
**Editorial director**: Kathy Middleton
**Production coordinator**: Margaret Salter
**Prepress technician**: Margaret Salter

**Logo design**: Samantha Crabtree
**Project Manager**: Santosh Vasudevan (Q2AMEDIA)
**Art Direction**: Rahul Dhiman (Q2AMEDIA)
**Design**: Neha Kaul (Q2AMEDIA)
**Illustrations**: Q2AMEDIA
**Front Cover**: Shuhei Nishida and Sueo Oe tie for 2nd and 3rd
   place in Olympic pole vaulting. Instead of having a jump
   off, the Japanese teammates decide to have two half-silver
   half-bronze medals created to share both positions.
**Title Page**: Shuhei Nishida and Sueo Oe on the Olympic podium

**Library and Archives Canada Cataloguing in Publication**

Hyde, Natalie, 1963-
   Live it: fairness / Natalie Hyde.

(Crabtree character sketches)
Includes index.
ISBN 978-0-7787-4883-0 (bound).--ISBN 978-0-7787-4916-5 (pbk.)

   1. Fairness--Juvenile literature. 2. Biography--Juvenile literature.
I. Title. II. Title: Fairness. III. Series: Crabtree character sketches

BJ1533.F2H93 2010        j179'.9        C2009-905422-1

**Library of Congress Cataloging-in-Publication Data**

Hyde, Natalie, 1963-
   Live it-- fairness / Natalie Hyde.
      p. cm. -- (Crabtree character sketches)
   Includes index.
   ISBN 978-0-7787-4916-5 (pbk. : alk. paper) -- ISBN 978-0-7787-4883-
(reinforced library binding : alk. paper)
1. Fairness--Juvenile literature. 2. Biography--Juvenile literature. I.
Title. II. Series.

   BJ1533.F3H93 2010
   179'.9--dc22

                              2009036007

# Crabtree Publishing Company

Printed in the USA/122009/BG20090930

www.crabtreebooks.com     1-800-387-7650

**Published in Canada**
**Crabtree Publishing**
616 Welland Ave.
St. Catharines, ON
L2M 5V6

**Published in the United States**
**Crabtree Publishing**
PMB 59051
350 Fifth Avenue, 59th Floor
New York, New York 10118

**Published in the United Kingdom**
**Crabtree Publishing**
Maritime House
Basin Road North, Hove
BN41 1WR

**Published in Australia**
**Crabtree Publishing**
386 Mt. Alexander Rd.
Ascot Vale (Melbourne)
VIC 3032

# CONTENTS

# WHAT IS FAIRNESS?

AT ONE TIME OR ANOTHER, WE'VE PROBABLY ALL SAID, "HEY! THAT'S NOT FAIR!" BUT WHAT DOES IT MEAN TO BE FAIR?

FAIRNESS MEANS PLAYING BY THE RULES. IT'S OFFERING ALL PEOPLE THE SAME OPPORTUNITIES. SOMETIMES FAIRNESS MEANS JUST DOING WHAT'S RIGHT. THE PEOPLE IN THIS BOOK ALL SHOWED WHAT FAIRNESS LOOKS LIKE. LET'S SEE WHAT THEY DID.

**MALLORY HOLTMAN AND LIZ WALLACE**
SOFTBALL PLAYERS

**SHUHEI NISHIDA AND SUEO OE**
OLYMPIC POLE VAULTERS FROM JAPAN

**ELSIE KNOTT**
CHIEF OF CURVE LAKE FIRST NATION,
ONTARIO, CANADA

**EDNA RUTH BYLER**
FOUNDER OF "TEN THOUSAND VILLAGES,"
A FAIR TRADE PROGRAM

**DR. WILFRED GRENFELL**
MEDICAL MISSIONARY

**MARGARET MARTIN**
FOUNDER OF THE HARMONY PROJECT

# FAIRNESS IN SPORTS

## MALLORY AND LIZ

**WHO ARE THEY?**
MEMBERS OF THE CENTRAL WASHINGTON WILDCATS SOFTBALL TEAM

**WHY THEM?**
THEY DECIDED FAIRNESS WAS MORE IMPORTANT THAN WINNING.

IN SPORTS, WE SOMETIMES FORGET THAT THERE ARE TWO TEAMS PLAYING. WE ONLY THINK ABOUT OUR OWN TEAM. TWO SOFTBALL PLAYERS SHOWED US THAT THIS WAY OF THINKING ISN'T ALWAYS FAIR. READ ON TO LEARN MORE ABOUT THEIR STORY.

THE CENTRAL WASHINGTON WILDCATS KNEW THEY NEEDED TO WIN THIS GAME AGAINST CENTRAL OREGON IN ORDER TO MOVE ON TO THE CHAMPIONSHIP.

WHAT DO YOU THINK, LIZ? CAN WE TAKE THIS TEAM?

WE'VE GOT A SHOT BUT IT WON'T BE EAS[Y]

AT THE TOP OF THE SECOND *INNING*, CENTRAL OREGON HAD TWO RUNNERS ON BASE. THEN SARA TUCHOLSKY CAME UP TO BAT.

LET'S GO WILDCATS! YOU CAN STRIKE HER OUT.

RA'S FIRST SWING
ON'T CONNECT.

THAT'S STRIKE ONE! LET'S KEEP IT GOING.

COME ON, SARA. THIS IS FOR A CHAMPIONSHIP SPOT!

BUT THEN...

WHAT A HIT!! RUN, SARA!!

GET THE BALL! OTHERWISE THEY'RE GOING TO GET THREE RUNS!

I CAN'T BELIEVE IT! MY FIRST EVER HOME RUN!

LOOK AT THAT!! A THREE-RUN [H]MER! SHE'S [N]EVER EVEN [D]ONE THAT [IN] PRACTICE!

BUT AS SHE HEADED TO SECOND, SARA REALIZED SHE HADN'T TOUCHED FIRST BASE. SHE STOPPED AND SPUN TO GO BACK...

OW! MY KNEE!

7

SARA'S HOME RUN WOULDN'T COUNT IF SHE COULDN'T MAKE IT AROUND THE BASES. BUT ACCORDING TO THE RULES, HER OWN TEAM COULDN'T HELP HER.

SARA, CAN YOU CRAWL BACK TO FIRST? THEN WE CAN PUT IN A *SUBSTITUTE* RUNNER.

I DON'T KNOW. IT HURTS SO MUCH.

SHE DESERVES THIS HOME RUN. SHE HIT IT OVER THE FENCE.

THEN MALLORY HAD AN IDEA.

HEY, UMPIRE. IS IT OKAY IF OUR TEAM HELPS HER?

SURE, THAT'S NOT AGAINST THE RULES. BUT ARE YOU SURE...?

MALLORY AND LIZ PICKED SARA UP AND BEGAN CARRYING HER AROUND THE BAS?

WHICH LEG IS HURT?

MY RIGHT LEG

OKAY, WE'RE GOING TO LOWER YOU A LITTLE, AND YOU TOUCH THE BASE WITH YOUR LEFT FOOT.

MALLORY AND LIZ LET SARA'S FOOT TOUCH EVERY BASE AS THEY WALKED HER AROUND THE *DIAMOND*.

THANK YOU SO MUCH!

YOU DESERVE IT. THAT WAS A BEAUTIFUL HIT.

IN 14 YEARS OF COACHING, I HAVE NEVER SEEN ANYTHING LIKE THAT.

SARAS'S THREE-RUN HOMER COST THE WILDCATS THE GAME AND THEIR CHANCE AT THE CHAMPIONSHIP. BUT NO ONE WAS SORRY.

SHE HIT THAT BALL FAIR AND SQUARE, COACH.

WELL, I'VE NEVER BEEN PROUDER OF MY TEAM.

MALLORY AND LIZ SHOWED THE TRUE MEANING OF SPORTSMANSHIP. EVEN KNOWING THEY MIGHT LOSE THE GAME, THEY STILL WANTED TO BE FAIR TO THE OTHER TEAM.

WHAT WOULD YOU DO?

YOUR TEAM IS IN THE FINALS OF A SOCCER TOURNAMENT. THE OTHER TEAM IS ONE PLAYER SHORT AND MAY HAVE TO FORFEIT. HOWEVER, YOU ARE ALLOWED TO LET ONE OF YOUR OWN PLAYERS PLAY WITH THE OTHER TEAM, IF YOU CHOOSE.

WOULD YOU LEND THE OTHER TEAM A PLAYER, OR WOULD YOU LET THEM FORFEIT?

## SHUHEI NISHIDA AND SUEO OE

**WHO ARE THEY?**
POLE VAULTERS AT THE 1936 BERLIN OLYMPICS

**WHY THEM?**
THEY TIED FOR SECOND PLACE AND FOUND A FAIR WAY TO SHARE THE ACCOMPLISHMENT.

SHUHEI AND SUEO BOTH TRAINED FOR YEARS TO COMPETE AT THE OLYMPICS. THEY TIED FOR SECOND PLACE, BUT ONLY ONE PERSON CAN WIN THE SILVER MEDAL. READ ON TO FIND OUT HOW THEY CREATED A FAIR SOLUTION.

THE MEN'S *POLE VAULT* EVENT AT THE 1936 OLYMPICS HAD BEEN GRUELING. BY CLEARING 3.8 METERS*, SHUHEI AND SUEO MADE IT TO THE FINAL ROUND, ALONG WITH THREE OTHER ATHLETES

THE AMERICANS ARE GOING TO BE TOUGH TO BEAT.

WE HAVE TO CONCENTRATE. WE'VE WORKED TOO HARD FOR THIS.

* APPROXIMATELY 12.5 FE

ENTUALLY, U.S. ATHLETE EARLE MEADOWS PTURED THE GOLD. THE THREE REMAINING EN WENT AFTER THE SILVER AND BRONZE. UHEI CLEARED THE BAR.

SHUHEI! SHUHEI!

THE OTHER Y DIDN'T MAKE ALL YOU NEED DO IS CLEAR E BAR AND WE LL BOTH HAVE A MEDAL.

BUT WE'VE BEEN AT THIS FOR HOURS! MY ARMS AND LEGS...

SUEO, YOU CAN DO THIS!

AND HE DID!

YOU DID IT! YOU DID IT! SUEO, THE SILVER AND BRONZE MEDALS ARE OURS!

BUT IT WASN'T THAT SIMPLE...

ITS BEEN NINE HOURS, AND THE TWO OF YOU ARE STILL TIED FOR SECOND PLACE. WE HAVE TO CONCLUDE THE COMPETITION.

HOW?

WITH A JUMP OFF. THE FIRST ONE NOT TO CLEAR THE BAR WILL GET THE BRONZE.

IT'S LATE AND WE'RE BOTH TIRED. IF WE JUMP NOW, NEITHER ONE OF US WILL BE DOING OUR BEST. IT ISN'T A FAIR WAY TO DECIDE.

SO HERE'S WHAT I THINK IS RIGHT. YOU JUMPED THE 4.15 METERS* ON YOUR FIRST TRY AND I DID IT ON MY SECOND. YOU TAKE SILVER.

* APPROXIMATELY 13.6 FEET

WE HAVE COME TO AN AGREEMENT. SHUHE WILL WIN SILVER.

AND SUEO WILL TAKE THE BRONZE.

THE *RECORD* BOOKS WILL SAY I WON SILVER AND YOU WON BRONZE, BUT IT DOESN'T FEEL FAIR. IN MY HEART, I WILL KNOW WE WERE EQUAL.

I HAVE AN IDEA HOW WE CAN SHOW THAT WE ARE SHARING THE MEDALS. I'LL TELL YOU WHE WE ARE HOME AGAIN.

...HOME IN JAPAN, THE TWO TEAMMATES ...K THEIR MEDALS TO A *JEWELER*.

YOU WANT ME TO DO WHAT?

CUT THE TWO MEDALS IN HALF ...D WELD THEM BACK ...GETHER, EACH ONE ...HALF SILVER AND HALF BRONZE.

IT'S ONLY FAIR. WE CLEARED THE SAME HEIGHT, SO NOW WE'LL HAVE THE SAME MEDAL!

THESE SPECIAL MEDALS ARE NOW KNOWN AS THE "MEDALS OF FRIENDSHIP."

BEING FAIR ISN'T ALWAYS EASY—ESPECIALLY WHEN THE WORLD IS WATCHING. BUT SHUHEI NISHIDA AND SUEO OE SHOWED WHAT FAIRNESS WAS WHEN THEY FIGURED OUT HOW TO SHARE THEIR OLYMPIC TITLE AND MEDALS.

DO YOU THINK YOU WOULD BE AS REASONABLE IN A SIMILAR SITUATION? LET'S FIND OUT!

## HAT WOULD YOU DO?

YOUR SCHOOL IS HOLDING A FUNDRAISING CONTEST. THE PERSON WHO SELLS THE MOST MAGAZINE SUBSCRIPTIONS WINS A STATE-OF-THE-ART GAMING SYSTEM. COMPETITION IS FIERCE!

THE RESULTS ARE POSTED. YOU AND ANOTHER STUDENT TIE FOR FIRST PLACE. WHAT IS A FAIR WAY FOR YOU TO SETTLE THIS?

## ELSIE KNOTT

**WHO WAS SHE?**
CHIEF OF CURVE LAKE FIRST NATION, ONTARIO, CANADA

**WHY HER?**
ELSIE KNOTT BELIEVED THAT NATIVE COMMUNITIES WERE NOT BEING TREATED FAIRLY. SHE DECIDED TO DO SOMETHING ABOUT IT.

ELSIE KNOTT WAS THE FIRST FEMALE CHIEF EVER ELECTED BY A FIRST NATION TRIBE. SHE WORKED HARD TO IMPROVE LIVING CONDITIONS AND OPPORTUNITIES FOR HER PEOPLE.

HOW DID ONE WOMAN ACCOMPLISH SO MUCH? READ ON TO FIND OUT.

ELSIE KNOTT WAS BORN IN 1916. AS A CHILD, SHE LIVED ON A NATIVE **RESERVE** AND ONLY WENT INTO TOWN ABOUT ONCE A YEAR.

LOOK AT ALL THE STORES, MAMA! THAT ONE OVER THERE SELLS NOTHING BUT CANDY!

THEY SEEM TO HAVE A STORE FOR EVERYTHING HERE.

IT'S SO DIFFERENT FROM THE RESERVE!

BUT THE RESERVE WAS ELSIE'S HOME. SHE MARRIED THERE AND HAD THREE CHILDREN. SHE WANTED TO MAKE LIFE BETTER FOR THEM. SO IN 1954...

I'M NOT SURE ANY WOMAN SHOULD BE CHIEF OF A FIRST NATION. WHY SHOULD I VOTE FOR YOU?

BECAUSE I'VE LIVED HERE ALL MY LIFE. I'M TIRED OF SEEING PEOPLE LIVING IN RUN-DOWN HOUSES AND HAVING NO DECENT EDUCATION, OR CLEAN WATER, OR PAVED ROADS. I'M GOING TO CHANGE ALL THAT.

ELSIE WON BY A LANDSLIDE

ETTER EDUCATION FOR NATIVE CHILDREN WAS ONE OF SIE'S TOP GOALS. SHE WAS WILLING TO DO ANYTHING O GET KIDS FROM THE RESERVE TO SCHOOL.

MRS. KNOTT, WHY IS OUR SCHOOL BUS A HEARSE THAT WAS USED FOR, YOU KNOW, DEAD PEOPLE?

BECAUSE THIS IS ALL WE COULD AFFORD. AND I HAD TO HAVE SOME WAY TO GET YOU TO SCHOOL. DOES IT MATTER?

WELL, SOME OF THE OTHER KIDS AT SCHOOL TEASE US ABOUT IT. WHY CAN'T THE BUS COME TO US?

HE'S RIGHT. IT'S JUST NOT FAIR THAT OUR COMMUNITY IS TREATED DIFFERENTLY THAN NON-NATIVE COMMUNITIES. THINGS HAVE GOT TO CHANGE.

SIE BEGAN WORKING HARDER THAN ER TO IMPROVE THE COMMUNITY.

IT'S ABOUT TIME YOU HAD PAVED ROADS HERE. MY BACK IS SORE FROM BUMPING ALONG IN MY TRUCK OVER POTHOLES.

WELL YOUR BACK ISN'T GOING TO GET A REST Y TIME SOON. ONCE YOUR GUYS ARE DONE PAVING THE ROADS, THEY CAN START DRILLING NEW WATER WELLS.

SHE ORGANIZED ALL KINDS OF FUNDRAISERS: DANCES, FISH FRIES, AND CORN ROASTS...

YOU NEVER STOP ELSIE! WHAT ARE WE RAISING MONEY FOR NOW?

I WANT TO START BOY SCOUTS AND GIRL GUIDE TROOPS FOR THE KIDS. THEY DESERVE TO HAVE FUN EARNING BADGES AND GOING TO *JAMBOREES*, TOO.

IN 1969, THE CANADIAN GOVERNMENT ATTEMPTED TO PASS A LAW THAT BECAME KNOWN AS THE "WHITE PAPER."

THEY'RE TRYING TO TAKE AWAY THE FEW RIGHTS WE HAVE AS NATIVE PEOPLE. THEY WANT US TO DISAPPEAR!

WELL, I'M NOT GOING TO LET THAT HAPPEN.

THE WHITE PAPER DIDN'T PASS. BUT ELSIE KNOTT NOW HAD A NEW *MISSION*: TO PRESERVE HER PEOPLE'S *HERITAGE*.

FIRST, SHE ADDED *OJIBWAY* LANGUAGE CLASSES IN THE SCHOOLS.

OKAY CLASS, I WANT TO BEGIN WORK ON RETELLING THE CREATION STORY FOR TOMORROW.

CAN'T WE JUST WRITE IT OUT FOR YOU?

MOST OF O STORIES WE HANDED DO ORALLY, TI SONGS AND STORYTELLIN ARE A BIG PA OF OUR CULTURE.

ELSIE ALSO *REINSTATED* THE ANNUAL CURVE LAKE *POWWOW*.

I'D FORGOTTEN HOW MUCH FUN A POWWOW WAS.

IT FEELS GOOD TO BRING BACK OUR TRADITIONS, DOESN'T IT?

BUT WHY [D]O YOU INVITE [T]HE WHITE [PE]OPLE TO OUR [P]OWWOW? [T]HIS IS OUR [C]ELEBRATION.

YES, BUT IF WE WANT OTHER PEOPLE TO UNDERSTAND US, THEY NEED TO SEE OUR CULTURE AND WAY OF LIFE. THEY NEED TO KNOW THAT WE ARE PEOPLE, JUST LIKE THEM.

MAYBE THEN THEY WILL ACT FAIRLY TOWARD US.

ELSIE KNOTT SHOWED THAT [F]AIR TREATMENT IS EVERYONE'S RIGHT. [THR]OUGH HER DEDICATION AND HARD WORK, [S]HE IMPROVED THE LIFE OF FIRST NATION PEOPLE ACROSS CANADA.

HOW WOULD YOU REACT IF YOU SAW OTHERS BEING TREATED UNFAIRLY? WOULD YOU BE WILLING TO TRY TO MAKE A CHANGE?

# [W]HAT WOULD YOU DO?

YOUR SCHOOL HAS ANNOUNCED THAT IT WILL BE ORGANIZING AN EXCITING ADVENTURE TRIP AT THE END OF THE YEAR. THE TRIP IS MEANT TO BUILD LEADERSHIP AND CONFIDENCE. IT ALSO COSTS $1000.

THIS UPSETS A LOT OF STUDENTS. WHAT IF SOME PEOPLE CAN'T AFFORD THE TRIP? IS IT REALLY FAIR THAT THEY DON'T HAVE THE SAME OPPORTUNITY AS STUDENTS WHO ARE ABLE TO AFFORD THE TRIP?

WHAT COULD YOU SUGGEST TO SCHOOL LEADERS THAT WOULD LET ALL STUDENTS HAVE A CHANCE TO TAKE PART IN THIS ADVENTURE?

## EDNA RUTH BYLER

**WHO IS SHE?**
A WORKER WITH THE MENNONITE CENTRAL COMMITTEE

**WHY HER?**
SHE FOUNDED "TEN THOUSAND VILLAGES," A FAIR TRADE ORGANIZATION.

EDNA BELIEVED IN HELPING OTHERS. THROUGH HER CHURCH, SHE AND HER HUSBAND VISITED COUNTRIES IN NEED OF HELP, AND DID WHATEVER THEY COULD. WHAT EDNA SAW ON ONE OF THOSE VISITS GAVE HER AN IDEA. KEEP READING TO FIND OUT WHAT IT WAS.

IN 1946, EDNA AND HER HUSBAND WENT ON A CHURCH MISSION TO PUERTO RICO.

DAVID WILL TAKE YOU TO ONE OF THE VILLAGES WE'RE WORKING WITH. SEE WHAT YOU CAN DO TO HELP.

I CAN'T BELIEVE THEY HAVE TO LIVE LIKE THIS.

I KNOW. AND LOOK AT THIS LITTLE GUY. HE'S SO THIN.

EDNA SUDDENLY HAD AN IDEA.

I'LL TAKE THESE BACK TO THE STATES WITH ME. MAYBE I CAN SELL THEM THERE!

WHERE DID YOU GET THESE? THEY'RE BEAUTIFUL!

THEY WERE MADE IN PUERTO RICO BY SOME VERY TALENTED WOMEN.

I'D LOVE TO BUY ONE. HOW MUCH DO THEY COST?

THE PRICE EDNA CHARGED WAS MUCH MORE THAN THE WOMEN WOULD HAVE RECEIVED FROM THEIR VILLAGE STORE. BUT IT WAS A FAIR PRICE FOR THE PEOPLE WHO WERE BUYING THE PRODUCTS.

LOOK HOW WELL-MADE THIS IS. YOU DON'T SEE HANDIWORK LIKE THIS ANYMORE.

IT WILL MAKE A PERFECT GIFT FOR MY SISTER.

OH! I'M TOO LATE, THEY'RE ALL GONE.

CAN YOU GET ANY MORE?

I'LL ORDER MORE RIGHT AWAY.

THE WOMEN IN THE VILLAGE WILL BE ABLE TO DO SO MUCH WITH THIS MONEY.

EDNA SENT BACK OFTEN FOR MORE ORDERS OF **NEEDLEWORK**. SHE SOON OPENED A STORE CALLED TEN THOUSAND VILLAGES, AND BEGAN TO BRING IN GOODS FROM OTHER COUNTRIES, AS WELL.

TEN THOUSAND VILLAGES STORE

WE JUST GOT ANOTHER ORDER FROM MRS. BYLER!

THESE ARE WONDERFUL! DO YOU HAVE MORE?

I NEVER THOUGHT WE WOULD SELL SO MANY PIECES.

WE'RE SOLD OUT OF THOSE, BUT I HAVE SOME BEAUTIFUL **CROSS-STITCH** FROM PAKISTAN.

AND AT SUCH A GOOD PRICE, I WILL FINALLY BE ABLE TO FIX MY ROOF!

TODAY, TEN THOUSAND VILLAGES STORES ACROSS NORTH AMERICA SELL HANDMADE PRODUCTS FROM OVER **60,000** ARTISANS FROM THIRD WORLD COUNTRIES.

THANKS TO EDNA BYLER, WHAT STARTED AS A WAY TO HELP A FEW WOMEN IN PUERTO RICO NOW HELPS PEOPLE FROM AROUND THE WORLD RECEIVE A FAIR PRICE FOR THEIR WORK.

## WHAT WOULD YOU DO?

A NEIGHBOR HIRES YOU TO DO SOME YARD WORK FOR HIM. YOU WORK REALLY HARD FOR TWO DAYS, DOING ALL KINDS OF CHORES. FINALLY, YOU FINISH ALL THE JOBS.

"HERE'S FIVE DOLLARS," SAYS YOUR NEIGHBOR. "THAT'S PRETTY GOOD MONEY FOR A KID YOUR AGE."

HOW CAN YOU POLITELY TELL YOUR NEIGHBOR THAT YOU DON'T FEEL YOU'VE BEEN PAID A FAIR WAGE FOR ALL THE WORK YOU DID?

# FAIRNESS IN HEALTH CARE

## DR. WILFRED GRENFELL

**WHO WAS HE?**
A MEDICAL MISSIONARY

**WHY HIM?**
HE HELPED PEOPLE IN REMOTE PLACES GET THE MEDICAL CARE THEY NEEDED.

IT'S EASY TO FORGET ABOUT PEOPLE WHO LIVE FAR AWAY FROM BIG CITIES. THEY OFTEN HAVE TO DO WITHOUT THINGS THAT CITY PEOPLE TAKE FOR GRANTED.

DR. WILFRED GRENFELL FELT IT WASN'T FAIR THAT SOME PEOPLE HAD NO WAY TO GET MEDICAL HELP BECAUSE OF WHERE THEY LIVED. READ ON TO FIND OUT HOW HE SOLVED THE PROBLEM.

WHEN DR. GRENFELL WAS A NEW DOCTOR, HIS FAVORITE TEACHER INSPIRED HIM TO JOIN *THE ROYAL NATIONAL MISSION TO DEEP SEA FISHERMEN.*

I KNOW IT LOOKS PRETTY BLEAK, BUT LABRADOR HAS A KIND OF WILD BEAUTY.

DO PEOPLE REALLY LIVE HERE YEAR-ROUND?

THEY SURE DO. WE CALL THEM 'LIVYERS.'

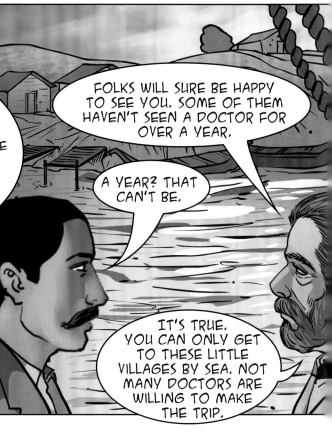

FOLKS WILL SURE BE HAPPY TO SEE YOU. SOME OF THEM HAVEN'T SEEN A DOCTOR FOR OVER A YEAR.

A YEAR? THAT CAN'T BE.

IT'S TRUE. YOU CAN ONLY GET TO THESE LITTLE VILLAGES BY SEA. NOT MANY DOCTORS ARE WILLING TO MAKE THE TRIP.

GRENFELL WAS SURPRISED BY THE POOR ...NG CONDITIONS OF THE LIVYERS.

ARE YOU SURE THIS IS THE PLACE? THAT ...HUT LOOKS TOO SMALL FOR A WHOLE FAMILY.

YES, IT'S THE PLACE. THEY HAVE NINE CHILDREN, AND I HEARD THE MOTHER HAS A CHEST INFECTION.

WE'RE GLAD TO SEE YOU, DOCTOR. MARY'S IN A BAD STATE.

HOW LONG HAS SHE BEEN ILL?

ABOUT THREE WEEKS NOW.

SHE'S GOT ...RONCHITIS. I'LL ...EAVE YOU SOME ...EDICINE AND A ...RM BLANKET. I'LL ...HECK BACK IN A ...OUPLE OF DAYS.

IS THE MEDICINE VERY EXPENSIVE? THE STORE OWNERS HERE CHARGE SO MUCH. THERE'S NEVER ANY MONEY LEFT...

DR. GRENFELL WANTED TO GIVE THEM THE MEDICINE, BUT HE KNEW THEY'D BE TOO PROUD TO TAKE HIS SERVICES FOR FREE.

THAT'S A BEAUTIFUL RUG YOUR WIFE HAS HOOKED. WHAT IF I TOOK THAT AS PAYMENT?

WOULD YOU REALLY DO THAT?

CERTAINLY. AND IF THERE IS ANY EXTRA MONEY, I'LL SEND BACK SOME SUPPLIES BY THE MAIL BOAT.

23

DR. GRENFELL TREATED MORE THAN **900** PATIENTS ON THAT TRIP. THE POVERTY HE SAW SHOCKED AND UPSET HIM.

THESE PEOPLE NEED MORE THAN ONE DOCTOR'S VISIT A YEAR. WITH BETTER CARE, WE COULD PREVENT A LOT OF SERIOUS ILLNESS. THERE MUST BE SOME WAY TO HELP.

DR. GRENFELL SPENT THE REST OF THAT YEAR RAISING MONEY.

THESE PEOPLE ALREADY LEAD VERY HARD LIVES. IS IT FAIR THAT THEY SHOULD ALSO SUFFER FROM LACK OF MEDICAL CARE?

THE NEXT SUMMER, DR. GRENFELL RETURNED TO LABRADOR WITH TWO OTHER DOCTORS AND TWO NURSES. THEY **ESTABLISHED** THE FIRST LABRADOR HOSPITAL AT BATTLE HARBOUR.

THIS HOSPITAL WILL REALLY MAKE A DIFFERENCE IN THESE PEOPLE'S LIVES.

AND WE'VE BEGUN TO BUILD A SECOND ONE IN INDIAN HARBOUR.

THEY ALSO BOUGHT A SECOND HOSPITAL SHIP, *THE PRINCESS MA* THAT YEAR, THEY TREATED NEAR **2,500** PATIENTS.

HERE, LET ME HELP YOU. AND THEN WE'LL SEE IF WE CAN MAKE THIS LITTLE ONE FEEL BETTER.

FOR 40 YEARS, DR. GRENFELL CONTINUED TO WORK TO IMPROVE THE LIVES OF THE PEOPLE OF LABRADOR. BY THE TIME HE RETIRED, HIS GRENFELL MISSION HAD...

BUILT TWO MORE HOSPITALS AND SEVEN NURSING STATIONS

SET UP SCHOOLS

BOUGHT 11 MORE HOSPITAL SHIPS

ESTABLISHED 14 INDUSTRIAL CENTERS

DR. GRENFELL WAS KNIGHTED IN 1927.

DR. GRENFELL DIDN'T FEEL IT WAS FAIR THAT SOME PEOPLE COULDN'T GET DECENT MEDICAL CARE. BUT HE DIDN'T JUST SHAKE HIS HEAD. HE DID SOMETHING ABOUT IT.

THERE ARE MANY SITUATIONS THAT JUST AREN'T FAIR. BUT IF YOU KNEW OF ONE, WOULD YOU DO MORE THAN FEEL BADLY ABOUT IT?

# WHAT WOULD YOU DO?

IMAGINE THAT A DANGEROUS FLU IS SPREADING ACROSS THE COUNTRY. A SHOT IS BEING OFFERED THAT COULD PREVENT PEOPLE FROM GETTING THE ILLNESS. BUT THE SHOT IS EXPENSIVE, AND MANY CAN'T AFFORD IT.

IS THIS SITUATION FAIR? WHAT DO YOU THINK SHOULD BE DONE?

# FAIRNESS OF OPPORTUNITY

## MARGARET MARTIN

**WHO IS SHE?**
A PUBLIC HEALTH WORKER

**WHY HER?**
SHE FOUNDED THE HARMONY PROJECT, A MUSIC PROGRAM FOR INNER-CITY CHILDREN.

MUSIC CAN DO MORE THAN SIMPLY ENTERTAIN PEOPLE. MUSIC CAN ALSO CHANGE LIVES. IT CAN GIVE PEOPLE CONFIDENCE, AND IT CAN OFFER KIDS A POSITIVE ACTIVITY IN PLACE OF A DANGEROUS ONE.

LET'S SEE HOW MARGARET MARTIN HELPED GIVE EVERY CHILD A FAIR CHANCE AT HAVING THIS OPPORTUNITY.

MARGARET MARTIN'S JOB AS A PUBLIC HEALTH WORKER TOOK HER INTO SOME OF THE POOREST SECTIONS OF LOS ANGELES.

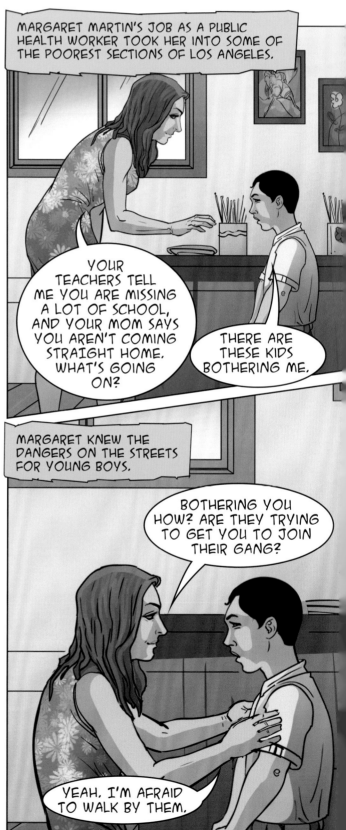

YOUR TEACHERS TELL ME YOU ARE MISSING A LOT OF SCHOOL, AND YOUR MOM SAYS YOU AREN'T COMING STRAIGHT HOME. WHAT'S GOING ON?

THERE ARE THESE KIDS BOTHERING ME.

MARGARET KNEW THE DANGERS ON THE STREETS FOR YOUNG BOYS.

BOTHERING YOU HOW? ARE THEY TRYING TO GET YOU TO JOIN THEIR GANG?

YEAH. I'M AFRAID TO WALK BY THEM.

I WISH I COULD HELP THESE KIDS MORE. BEING OUT ON THE STREETS WITH NOTHING TO DO MAKES THEM AN EASY TARGET FOR GANGS. AND ONCE THEY'RE IN A GANG...

OH, NO! WHAT ARE THEY GOING TO DO TO THAT POOR KID? ROB HIM?

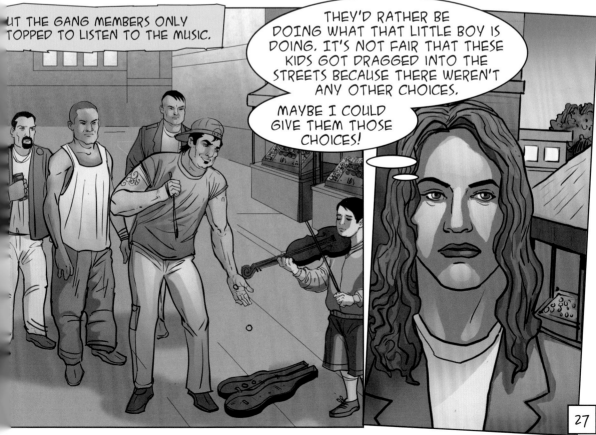

...UT THE GANG MEMBERS ONLY ...TOPPED TO LISTEN TO THE MUSIC.

THEY'D RATHER BE DOING WHAT THAT LITTLE BOY IS DOING. IT'S NOT FAIR THAT THESE KIDS GOT DRAGGED INTO THE STREETS BECAUSE THERE WEREN'T ANY OTHER CHOICES.

MAYBE I COULD GIVE THEM THOSE CHOICES!

27

MARGARET KNEW SHE'D NEED HELP GETTING HER PROJECT OFF THE GROUND.

IF THE *ROTARY* CAN HELP FUND THIS, I THINK I CAN MAKE A DIFFERENCE. WE'LL GIVE THE KIDS INSTRUMENTS AND FREE LESSONS. WE'LL GIVE THEM AN ALTERNATIVE TO GANGS.

I THINK IT'S A BRILLIANT IDEA. LET'S MAKE IT HAPPEN!

MARGARET WENT TO SCHOOLS IN SOME OF THE POOREST NEIGHBORHOODS.

THE HARMONY PROJECT IS A NEW PROGRAM. WE WILL GIVE FREE MUSIC LESSONS AND FREE INSTRUMENTS FOR YOU TO USE. AND YOU'LL ALSO HAVE A SAFE PLACE TO GO AFTER SCHOOL.

THIS SOUNDS GREAT! I'M GOING TO SIGN UP.

SOON, THE FIRST CLASSES WERE UNDERWAY.

OKAY, LET'S MAKE MUSIC!

I LOVE COMING HERE. NO ONE BOTHERS ME LIKE BEFORE. AND WHEN I'M FEELING MAD OR *FRUSTRATED*, I PLAY AND IT REALLY HELPS ME.*

I KNOW, ME TOO.

*ACTUAL QUOTE

I NEVER THOUGHT IT WOULD GROW SO BIG SO FAST, BUT WHAT A DIFFERENCE IT HAS MADE IN THESE KIDS' LIVES!

NOW, WE NEED TO DO THIS IN EVERY BIG CITY IN THE COUNTRY. THINK OF ALL THE KIDS WHO WILL HAVE A CHANCE TO LOVE MUSIC!

TODAY THE HARMONY PROJECT PROVIDES INSTRUMENTS AND YEAR-ROUND MUSIC LESSONS TO MORE THAN SEVEN HUNDRED KIDS, AND THE PROJECT IS STILL GROWING!

MARGARET MARTIN FOUND THAT PROVIDING KIDS WITH REAL CHOICES MADE THE WORLD JUST A LITTLE MORE FAIR. WHAT IF MORE PEOPLE THOUGHT LIKE SHE DID?

## WHAT WOULD YOU DO?

IT'S ALMOST IMPOSSIBLE TO IMAGINE THE WORLD WITHOUT COMPUTERS. PEOPLE USE THEM TO NETWORK WITH FRIENDS, DO THEIR WORK, AND FIND INFORMATION. BUT NOT EVERY PERSON HAS ONE.

YOU KNOW THIS ISN'T FAIR. KIDS WHO DON'T HAVE ACCESS TO COMPUTERS ARE GOING TO BE LEFT BEHIND. CAN YOU THINK OF A WAY TO GET COMPUTERS TO THOSE WHO NEED THEM? THINK BIG! MARGARET MARTIN DID.

# WEB SITES

GO TO THIS SITE TO LEARN ALL ABOUT THE OLYMPICS.

www.olympic.org

READ MORE ABOUT THE HISTORY AND MISSION OF TEN THOUSAND VILLAGES.

www.tenthousandvillages.com

VIEW ACTUAL PICTURES OF DR. GRENFELL AND THE GRENFELL MISSION.

http://collections.mun.ca/cdm4/browse.php?CISOROOT=%2Fm_grenfell

SEE HOW THE HARMONY PROJECT CONTINUES TO HELP COMMUNITIES.

www.harmony-project.org

# GLOSSARY

**BRONCHITIS** INFLAMMATION OF THE LUNGS

**CROSS-STITCH** A TYPE OF EMBROIDERY

**DIAMOND** IN BASEBALL, THE AREA OUTLINED BY THE FOUR BASES ON THE FIELD

**ESTABLISHED** MADE HAPPEN

**FRUSTRATED** UPSET AND ANNOYED

**HANDIWORK** SOMETHING A PERSON MAKES

**HERITAGE** SOMETHING HANDED DOWN FROM EARLIER GENERATIONS

**HOMER** A HOME RUN IN BASEBALL

**INNING** A SINGLE TURN AT BAT FOR A TEAM

**JAMBOREES** A LARGE RALLY OF BOY SCOUTS OR GIRL SCOUTS

**JEWELER** SOMEONE WHO MAKES JEWELRY, AND CAN ALSO REPAIR DELICATE OBJECTS

**MISSION** AN ASSIGNMENT CARRIED OUT FOR RELIGIOUS OR POLITICAL REASONS

**NEEDLEWORK** A SPECIAL TYPE OF SEWING

**OJIBWAY** NORTH AMERICAN TRIBE NEAR LAKE SUPERIOR

**POLE VAULT** AN EVENT WHERE ATHLETES JUMP OVER A BAR WITH A LONG, FLEXIBLE POLE

**POWWOW** A NATIVE NORTH AMERICAN CEREMONY

**RECORD** AN OFFICIAL REPORT OF AN ACHIEVEMENT

**REINSTATED** PUT BACK

**RESERVE** LAND SET ASIDE FOR NATIVE PEOPLE TO LIVE ON (CANADIAN)

**ROTARY** A WORLDWIDE CHARITABLE SOCIETY

**SUBSTITUTE** IN SPORTS, A PLAYER PUT IN TO TAKE ANOTHER'S PLACE

# INDEX